THE GREATEST SPORTS TRIVIA BOOK OF ALL TIME

Over 800 Trivia Questions, Answers, Sports Stats, And Fun Facts

STEVE FALVEY

First edition 2022.

DEDICATION

This book is dedicated to my dad, Mark. The endless trainings, game days, celebrations and comiserations were all better with you. I loved when you'd watch me play and I loved the chats afterwards and all the chats since. Our conversations about sport are still one of the more enjoyable things we ever discuss. I love you, dad.

TABLE OF CONTENTS

INTRODUCTION

Sport is one of the greatest unifiers on the planet. There is a reason that college football games quickly become turf wars, why we stand and cheer more when the Ice Titans drop the gloves than when they score, and why every four years we are glued to the television to watch the incredible feats of humankind at the Olympic Games. We love the stunning victories, the feel-good stories and the underdog spirit that sport allows us to witness.

Growing up in Australia, I was raised on a steady diet of meat and two vegetables with a side of whatever sport was happening and on television at the time. From cricket to rugby, soccer to athletics, college to pro, it didn't matter, I was obsessed. Later in life, I moved to the USA and saw and experienced first-hand the bright lights of sporting coliseums, where every kid dreams of being a champion at one point in their life.

No matter how much sport I was exposed to, I hungered for more. I would research the players, the coaches and even the fan bases of these world-famous clubs and teams. The deeper my research got the more I realised that I wasn't alone in my pursuit of the facts and stats that drive these games and sports from within. There is a term for people like me and if you're reading this book, I suspect you may suffer from the same condition; it's called being a fanatic.

From one fanatic to another, I hope you enjoy this sports trivia book that will take you from the excellence and professionalism of the US sporting juggernaut to the Olympics, to college sportsfields and more. It will also throw in a few fun sports that are only played in certain parts of the world, just for the fun of it.

SECTION 1

QUESTIONS

Will you be the sports trivia G.O.A.T?

CHAPTER 1

BASKETBALL

Trivia Questions

1. Which legendary NBA player is known as the 'Black Mamba'?
2. How many times was Michael Jordan crowned the MVP of the NBA?
3. Which two teams played in the first ever NBA game?
4. What is the real given name of Magic Johnson?
5. When was the 3-point shot introduced to the NBA?
6. What is Kevin Garnett's nickname?
7. When did the WNBA (Women's National Basketball Association) commence?

8. How many teams did Larry Bird play for in the NBA?

9. As of 2021, how many NBA teams have not won a championship?

10. Who is the only player to ever score 100 points in an NBA game?

11. Manu Ginobili is from which country?

12. Who is the player depicted on the NBA logo?

13. Which two teams were playing when the infamous 'Malice at The Palace' incident occurred?

14. In the NBA finals in 1997 which iconic player dropped 38 points in what has been labelled 'The Flu Game'?

15. When was the first NBA game played?

16. Which 12-time NBA all-star from the Detroit Pistons walked off the court during the finals against the Chicago Bulls, resulting in long-standing beef with Michael Jordan?

17. Who was the first ever NBA player to be enshrined?

18. Who has the most coaching titles in the NBA?

19. What is Kareem Abdul-Jabbar's birth name?

20. Who was the #1 draft pick in 2003?

21. Which team drafted the legendary all-star Ray Allen?

22. Who has played the most career NBA games?

23. Bob Pettit was the first ever NBA what?

24. Who is the first player to be drafted #1 without playing college or high school basketball in the US?

25. As of 2021, how many players have played for 12 teams or more?

26. Which NBA team has the most wins? (As of 2022)

27. What team has the most playoff appearances?

28. Stephen Curry led all rookies in which category for the 2009-10 NBA season?

29. Who passed Kobe Bryant as the leading scorer in NBA all-star history?

30. An NBA basketball game has 4 quarters of how many minutes each?

31. Crypto.com Arena in LA used to be known as what?

32. Who owns the Charlotte Hornets (2022)?

33. Who was the first person to win NBA MVP, NBA Coach of the Year, and NBA Executive of the Year?

34. How many players does an NBA team have on its roster?

35. How many NBA stadiums are there?

36. Which country was Steve Nash born in?

37. Which player did the Los Angeles Lakers give up for Kobe Bryant?

38. Which city was the famous Dallas Maverick, Dirk Nowitzki, from?

39. Who was the first foreign player to be drafted #1 overall?

40. What type of ball was Basketball originally played with?

41. Which musical artist sold his ownership share in the Brooklyn Nets in 2013?

42. Who is the only player in NBA history to have 3 sons play in the league?

43. Which expansion team was the first to win the NBA finals?

44. Which team was the first to sweep the NBA finals?

45. Who was the first high school player to go straight to the league and get drafted first overall?

46. What city were the Golden State Warriors initially from?

47. Which year was the 24-second shot clock introduced?

48. Who played every position in an NBA finals game in his rookie year?

49. What was the most famous nickname for Sam Perkins?

50. Which player over 7 feet tall has won championships with both Los Angeles Lakers and Miami Heat?

Match the players with the institution they were drafted from

Player	Institution
Lebron James	North Carolina University
Kobe Bryant	University of Connecticut
Larry Bird	Harlem Globetrotters
Charles Barkley	University of Oklahoma
Lamelo Ball	University of Texas
Michael Jordan	UCLA
Dennis Rodman	DJK Wurzburg
Steve Nash	Georgetown
Tim Duncan	Kansas Jayhawks
Wilt Chamberlain	Kentucky Wildcats
Kevin Garnett	Farragut Career Academy High School
Blake Griffin	Arizona State University

Jerry West	Marquette University
Shaquille O'Neal	FC Barcelona
James Harden	Auburn
Giannis Antetokounmpo	Southeastern Oklahoma State
Dwayne Wade	University of Utah
Pau Gasol	Duke Blue Devils
Reggie Miller	Indiana State
Ray Allen	Wake Forest
Allen Iverson	LSU Tigers
Dirk Nowitzki	West Virginia University
Kevin Durant	Filathlitikos
Andrew Bogut	Lower Merion High School
Ben Simmons	Louisiana State University
Joel Embiid	St Vincent – St Mary High School
Devin Booker	Illawarra Hawks
Jayson Tatum	Santa Clara University

Unbelievable Statistics and Records

1. **Wilt Chamberlain** played every minute of every game, including overtime, (except for a total of 8 minutes) during the 1961 – 1962 season. The top seven spots in minutes-per-game in NBA history are all held by Chamberlain.

2. **Giff Roux** of the St Louis Bombers once missed 20 consecutive free throws in 1948. His team lost that game by only 4 points.

3. In a game in which you are fouled out after 6 personal fouls, **Cal Bowdler** of the Atlanta Hawks committed 7 personal fouls during a game in 1999.

4. The great **Wilt Chamberlain** has, perhaps, one of the most unbreakable NBA records: 118 50-point games. This achievement is almost 4 times the number belonging to the player who occupies the second spot on the list; Michael Jordan.

5. **Bill Russell**, the 5-time league MVP, holds the record for the most NBA championships as a player, with 11 in total. It's hard to imagine that a player in the modern game will ever supersede this.

6. **Klay Thompson** of the Golden State Warriors holds the record for the most points in a single quarter. Scoring 37 points against the Sacramento Kings in 2015 was a monumental effort, and beat the previous record of 33 points in a quarter.

7. **Bubba Wells** of the Dallas Mavericks holds, perhaps, one of the worst records in NBA history. Going up against Dennis Rodman, Wells was fouled out of the game in 2 minutes and 43 seconds; the quickest disqualification in history.

8. More often than not, 107 points would be a winning score in the NBA. In 1990, the **Phoenix Suns** put up that number in just 1 half of basketball. They went on to score 173 points for the game, defeating the Boston Celtics, who still managed to score 143 points, themselves.

9. The **Chicago Bulls** juggernaut of the 1990s attracted a crowd in every city they played in. However, on one occasion in 1998 against Atlanta, the Bulls and Hawks drew a crowd of 62 046 people in the Georgia Dome.

10. In 2012, Orlando Magic star, **Dwight Howard**, attempted 39 free throws in a single game. A little over a year later, he attempted the same number, but this time playing against the Magic for the Lakers. Howard improved his percentage, as his first attempt made 21 free throws and his second, 25. The rules for fouling off the ball have since been changed, meaning that the record is likely to go unbroken.

Match the teams with their owners

Team	Owner
Chicago Bulls	Michael Jordan
Dallas Mavericks	Dan DeVos
Charlotte Hornets	Tilman Fertitta
Indiana Pacers	Jerry Reinsdorf
Portland Trailblazers	Mark Cuban
Orlando Magic	Ann Walton Kronke
New Orleans Pelicans	Dan Gilbert
Brooklyn Nets	Tom Gores
Cleveland Cavaliers	Gayle Benson
Houston Rockets	Jody Allen
Denver Nuggets	Herbert Simon
Detroit Pistons	Joseph Tsai

CHAPTER 2

BASEBALL

Trivia Questions

1. Who wore the famous #7 for the New York Yankees?

2. What year was the iconic 'Field of Dreams' game?

3. In the 2012 season, Carlos Beltran became the first switch hitter to hit 300 homers and do what?

4. Who is baseball's 'Mr November'?

5. Babe Ruth played during what years?

6. Who was the first pitcher to throw a Major League 'no-hitter'?

7. 1903 had the first what in baseball?

8. What was the original name of the Boston Braves?

9. Which pitcher has allowed the most home runs in MLB?

10. Which Major League stadium has the highest crowd capacity?

11. Which is the oldest baseball team in the USA?

12. Who was the first ever player to have their number retired?

13. Which year was Aaron Judge the Rookie of the Year?

14. The Milwaukee Brewers were originally from where?

15. Which NBA MVP is a part owner of the Boston Red Sox?

16. Who was the first player to hit a Major League home run?

17. True or False? Archie 'Moonlight' Graham (made famous in the iconic movie, Field of Dreams) was a real-life baseball player, and actually played a single game for the New York Giants in 1905.

18. How many grand slams did Derek Jeter hit during his career?

19. What color is the stitching on a Major League Baseball?

20. The Cincinnati Reds were known by what nickname?

21. Which player has won the National League MVP seven times?

22. How many games are in an MLB regular season?

23. Who was the first woman in the Baseball Hall of Fame?

24. Who won the 2012 World Series?

25. Which team won two World Series in the 2000s?

26. What was Hall of Fame umpire John Conlon's nickname?

27. Who was the first player to hit 50 home runs and 50 doubles in a season?

28. Which batter was the first to strike out 2500 times?

29. Who was the first player to ever become a part of the '500 club'?

30. Which pitcher won 16 Golden Glove awards?

31. How many different ways are there for a batter to reach first base?

32. Which was the first Major League baseball team to call Seattle its hometown?

33. Who hit the very first World Series home run at Yankee Stadium in 1923?

34. Whitey Ford played his entire career with which team?

35. Hank Aaron retired from the sport from which team?

36. The New York Mets won their first World Series in which year?

37. In 1892, who became the first team to win 100 games in a season?

38. Before becoming the San Francisco Giants, what was the team called?

39. Who led the 2002 Chicago Cubs in home runs?

40. Which pitcher threw the first ever perfect game in a World Series?

41. What was the Angels' inaugural year?

42. What is the unofficial anthem for American Baseball?

43. Who is the youngest player elected to the Hall of Fame?

44. Who holds the record for the fastest baseball pitch by a woman at 69 mph? (As of 2022)

45. In the movie 'Field of Dreams', John Kinsella (Ray Kinsella's father) wears the uniform of which team?

46. Which team moved to Washington D.C. to become the Washington Nationals?

47. Cal Ripken Jr. holds the record for what in baseball?

48. Who is the oldest pitcher in MLB history?

49. How many seams are on a baseball?

50. Jackie Robinson is most famous for what?

Match the Major League team (MLB) with their former stadium

Stadium Name	Team
The Ballpark in Arlington	Philadelphia Phillies
Turner Field	Seattle Mariners
Memorial Stadium	St Louis Cardinals
Ebbets Field	San Francisco Giants
Comiskey Park	Texas Rangers
Veterans Stadium	Pittsburgh Pirates
Three Rivers Stadium	Atlanta Braves
Busch Memorial Stadium	Baltimore Orioles
Candlestick Park	Chicago White Sox
Kingdome	New York Mets
Griffith Stadium	Brooklyn Dodgers
Shea Stadium	Washington Senators

Hollywood at the ballpark:
Match the movie with the Baseball team

Movie Title	Team
61*	Chicago White Sox
For Love of the Game	Tampa Bay Devil Rays
The Rookie	Oakland A's
Moneyball	Atlanta Braves
42	New York Yankees
Major League	New York Knights
The Natural	Chicago Cubs
Rookie of the Year	Cleveland Indians
Trouble with the Curve	Brooklyn Dodgers
Field of Dreams	Detroit Tigers

True or False?

1. Ron Hunt is the only 20th century player to be hit by a pitch 50 times in a season.

2. Minnie Monoso's career spanned 5 decades.

3. Walter Alston has the highest win percentage of any manager who has a minimum of 1000 games under their belt.

4. The Philadelphia Phillies were once called the 'Perfectos'.

5. In the 1990s, the LA Dodgers had 5 Rookie of the Year awards.

6. Jim Abbott played for 10 years in the major league; is it true he only had one hand?

7. Derek Jeter holds the record for most double plays by a short stop.

8. Alex Rodriguez holds the record for being hit by pitches the most in the modern game.

9. Clayton Kershaw won the MVP and Cy Young Award in the same year.

10. 70 is the average number of baseballs used in a major league game.

Famous Players' Jerseys - Best of their number

0 - Texas Rangers (1978) - Al Oliver

2 - New York Yankees (1995 - 2014) - Derek Jeter

4 - New York Yankees (1923 - 1939) - Lou Gehrig

6 - St. Louis Cardinals (1941 - 1963) - Stan Musial

8 - Baltimore Orioles (1981 - 2001) - Cal Ripken Jr.

10 - Atlanta Braves (1993 - 2012) - Chipper Jones

11 - Cincinnati Reds (1986 - 2004) - Barry Larkin

16 - New York Yankees (1950 - 1967) - Whitey Ford

17 - Colorado Rockies (1997 - 2013) - Todd Helton

19 - San Diego Padres (1982 - 2001) - Tony Gwynn

22 - Los Angeles Dodgers (2008 - 2022*) - Clayton Kershaw

25 - Pittsburgh Pirates & San Francisco Giants (1986 - 2007) - Barry Bonds

39 - Brooklyn Dodgers (1948 - 1957) - Roy Campanella

42 - Brooklyn Dodgers (1947 - 1956) - Jackie Robinson

49 - New York Yankees (1975 - 1988) - Ron Guidry

59 - Cleveland Indians (2009 - 2022*) Carlos Carrasco

79 - Chicago White Sox - (2014 - 2022*) Jose Aubrey

99 - New York Yankees - (2016 - 2022*) Aaron Judge

CHAPTER 3

AMERICAN FOOTBALL

Trivia Questions

1. Which team has won the most Super Bowls? (As of 2022)
2. What does 'NFL' stand for?
3. Peyton Manning joined the Denver Broncos in 2012. Which team did he play for before that?
4. How many seasons did Peyton Manning play with the Colts?
5. How many NFL teams has controversial wide receiver Antonio Brown played for? (As of 2022)
6. Which was the highest-scoring game in NFL history?
7. What are the two conferences that make up the NFL?

8. Which is the only NFL team to have completed a perfect (regular) season?
9. The New York Jets used to be known as what?
10. Who was the first player to be drafted into the NFL?
11. When did the New Orleans Saints last win a Super Bowl?
12. Robert Griffin III held a passer rating of what in 2012?
13. Marvin Gaye famously tried out for which NFL franchise in 1970?
14. Jerry Rice holds what record in his career?
15. When was the first Super Bowl ever played?
16. How many teams are in the NFL?
17. Dan Marino was an all-star quarterback for which team?
18. Which player famously took a knee in 2016 in protest against police brutality?
19. Tim Tebow played for which NFL teams in his career?
20. True or False? the Dayton Triangles was once an NFL team.
21. Who was the highest paid player in the NFL in 2021?
22. What was the longest field goal ever made by an NFL kicker?
23. Which NFL franchise began playing its home games at the Hubert H. Humphrey Metrodome in 1982?
24. Which franchise has played in LA, St Louis, and Cleveland?
25. The Indianapolis Colts originally joined the NFL under what name?

26. Which city did the Washington Commanders originally play in as the Braves?

27. In which year did the Cincinnati Bengals join the NFL?

28. How many teams played in the inaugural NFL season in 1922?

29. The Tennessee Titans played in which city for one season, before taking up their permanent residence in Nashville?

30. Pete Carroll coached which team to a super bowl championship in 2014?

31. Who owns the Dallas Cowboys?

32. NFL tackle, Michael Oher, was the feature of which Hollywood blockbuster starring Sandra Bullock?

33. Which player is credited with changing the way linebackers and pass rushing are played?

34. Which team carries the nickname, ‘America’s Team’?

35. The Detroit Lions started out with what name?

36. Which NFL franchise was the first to reach 700 wins?

37. Which team’s defence had the nickname ‘Blitz Inc’ from 1999 – 2004?

38. Jim Brown played for which team when he rushed for 10 000 rushing yards?

39. Kyler Murray was the number 1 draft pick in 2019, selected by which franchise?

40. How many days was Tom Brady retired in 2022?

Match the players with their teams

Player	Team
Myles Garrett	Indianapolis Colts
Sam Bradford	Tampa Bay Buccaneers
Steve Emtman	Cleveland Browns
Jadeveon Clowney	New England Patriots
Bo Jackson	Los Angeles Rams
O.J. Simpson	Dallas Cowboys
Kenneth Sims	St Louis Rams
Terry Bradshaw	Houston Texans
Troy Aikman	Buffalo Bills
Billy Cannon	Pittsburgh Steelers

Match the players with their nicknames

Player	Nickname
'Minister of Defense'	John Unitas
'The Golden Arm'	Red Grange
'Sweetness'	Deion Sanders
'Joe Cool'	Marshawn Lynch
'Night Train'	Reggie White
'The Galloping Ghost'	Joe Montana
'Mercury'	William Perry
'Prime Time'	Don Hutson
'Ironhead'	Tyrann Mathieu
'Broadway Joe'	Eugene Morris
'Honey Badger'	Joe Namath
'Beast Mode'	Jim Kelly
'The Refrigerator'	Walter Payton
'Machine Gun'	Craig Heyward
'The Alabama Antelope'	Dick Lane

Match the celebrities with the teams they root for

Celebrity	Team
Blake Shelton	Cincinnati Bengals
Samuel L. Jackson	Kansas City Chiefs
Michael Phelps	Cleveland Browns
Shooter McGavin	Atlanta Falcons
Stephen 'Steph' Curry	Green Bay Packers
Barack Obama	Denver Broncos
George Clooney	Indianapolis Colts
Elvis Presley	Baltimore Ravens
Demi Lovato	Houston Texans
Jessica Biel	Jacksonville Jaguars
Eminem	Arizona Cardinals
Ellen DeGeneres	Chicago Bears
Simone Biles	Detroit Lions
Rob Lowe	Carolina Panthers
Bill Murray	Dallas Cowboys
Paul Rudd	Buffalo Bills

Celebrity	Team
Ice Cube	Miami Dolphins
Chuck Liddell	Minnesota Vikings
Ty Burrell	New Orleans Saints
Johnny Depp	San Francisco 49ers
Josh Duhamel	Philadelphia Eagles
Mark Wahlberg	New York Jets
Brad Pitt	Seattle Seahawks
Hugh Jackman	Tennessee Titans
Ray Romano	Los Angeles Rams
Kevin Hart	Washington Football Team
Frank Sinatra	Las Vegas Raiders
Jeremy Renner	Pittsburgh Steelers
J.K. Rowling	Tampa Bay Buccaneers
John Cena	New York Giants
Faith Hill & Tim McGraw	New England Patriots
Matthew McConaughey	Los Angeles Chargers

Unbreakable Records

1. **Derrick Thomas** – 7 Sacks in one game for the Kansas City Chiefs, against the Seattle Seahawks in 1990, Week 10.

2. **Marvin Harrison** – 143 receptions in 2002 for the Indianapolis Colts; the closest to Harrison's mark had 31 fewer catches for the season.

3. **Tampa Bay Buccaneers** – 26 straight losses.

4. **George Blanda** – 26 NFL seasons.

5. **Brett Favre** – 297 straight games at quarterback. Favre took over in 1992, and played 16 seasons in Greenbay before playing one for the Jets and two more with the Vikings.

CHAPTER 4

ICE HOCKEY

Trivia Questions

1. Who is known for being the first player to play with a curved stick blade?
2. Who did the Anaheim Mighty Ducks play in their first ever game?
3. Which home team was the first to win an NHL Winter Classic?
4. When was the NHL founded?
5. As of 2020, how many teams have never won a Stanley Cup?
6. How many Stanley Cups has Wayne Gretzky won?
7. Who is the highest scoring goalie in NHL history?
8. Which country do the most NHL players originate from?

9. Where is the Hockey Hall of Fame situated?
10. How does an NHL Hockey game begin?
11. What is the name of the penalty that occurs when a player hits an opposing player with their stick?
12. Which band is famously named after the penalty given to a player for fighting?
13. The Vezina Trophy is awarded to who?
14. What does a 'Gordie Howe hat trick' consist of?
15. 'Hooking' refers to what?
16. How long can the goalkeeper hold the puck for?
17. Who was the first player of color in the NHL?
18. From 2021, which is the most recent team to join the NHL?
19. Who was the first NHL commissioner?
20. Who was known as 'The Golden Jet'?
21. In what year was the offside rule introduced by the NHL?
22. Which team was the first to ever win back-to-back Stanley Cup titles?
23. Which NHL team once drafted a player that didn't exist?
24. What was the longest shootout in NHL history?

25. What was the name of the player who once ripped off a fan's shoe and beat him with it?

26. Jeremy Roenick wore what number for the Phoenix Coyotes?

27. In what year was Alex Ovechkin drafted?

28. True or False? The NHL uses frozen pucks to prevent the puck from bouncing during play.

29. Which typing errors does the Stanley Cup contain?

30. Which team once famously threw the Stanley Cup into a fire?

31. How many players have won the Stanley Cup and an Olympic gold medal in the same season?

Match the A-listers with the teams they root for

Celebrity	Team they support
Will Ferrell, Cuba Gooding Jr	Detroit Red Wings
Justin Bieber	Los Angeles Kings
Celine Dion	Chicago Blackhawks
Kristen Bell	Winnipeg Jets
Tim Robbins	Montreal Canadiens
Alice Cooper	Washington Capitals
Metallica	Buffalo Sabres
Chad Michael Murray	New York Islanders
Vince Vaughn	New York Rangers
Brett Kissell	San Jose Sharks
Chris Jericho	Toronto Maple Leafs
Russell Crowe	Edmonton Oilers
Billy Joel	Boston Bruins
Larry King	Pittsburgh Penguins
Adam Sandler	Arizona Coyotes

Celebrity	Team they support
Evander Holyfield	Florida Panthers
Keith Urban, Carrie Underwood	Carolina Hurricanes
Dwayne "The Rock" Johnson	St Louis Blues
Stephen King	Seattle Kraken
John Elway	Ottawa Senators
Patrick Mahomes	Anaheim Ducks
Gordon Ramsay	Colorado Avalanche
Katy Perry	Nashville Predators
Michael Buble	Minnesota Wild
Jason Momoa	Vancouver Canucks
Macklemore	New Jersey Devils
Erin Andrews	Columbus Blue Jackets
George W. Bush	Vegas Golden Knights
Milo Ventimiglia	Philadelphia Flyers
Kate Hudson	Dallas Stars
Matthew Perry	Minnesota Wild
Sylvester Stallone	Tampa Bay Lightning

Unbreakable Records

1. **Dave Williams:** Most Career Penalty Minutes – 3966 penalty minutes.
2. **Martin Brodeur:** Most Career Wins by a Goalie – 691.
3. **Doug Jarvis:** Most Consecutive Games – 964 games.
4. **Gordie Howe:** Oldest Player – 52 years 11 days.
5. **Bill Mosienko:** Fastest Hat Trick by a Single Person – 21 seconds.
6. **Wayne Gretzky:** Most Career Points – 2857.
7. **Montreal Canadiens:** Most Consecutive Stanley Cup Finals Appearances – 10 consecutive times.
8. **Henri Richard:** Most Career Stanley Cup Wins as a Player – 11.

Best NHL Chirps

1. "We get nose jobs all the time in the NHL, and we don't even have to go to the hospital." – Hall of Fame defenseman, **Brad Park**.
2. "All hockey players are bilingual; they speak English and profanity." – **Gordie Howe**.
3. "Half the game is mental; the other half is being mental." – Former Maple Leaf, **Jim McKenny**.
4. [Ice hockey is] "a fast, body-contact game played by men with clubs in their hands and knives laced to their feet." – **Paul Gallico**.
5. "Every day you guys look worse and worse. And today, you played like tomorrow." – **John Mariucci**, to his U.S. Hockey team.
6. "Ice hockey is a form of disorderly conduct in which the score is kept." – **Doug Larson**.
7. "How would you like a job where, every time you make a mistake, a big red light goes on, and 18,000 people boo?" – **Jacques Plante**.
8. "High sticking, tripping, slashing, spearing, charging, hooking, fighting, unsportsmanlike conduct, interference, roughing… everything else is just figure skating." – **Scotty Bowman**.
9. "Hockey players wear numbers because you can't always identify the body with dental records." – **Bob Plager**.

10. “Street hockey is great for kids. It’s energetic, competitive, and skilful. And best of all, it keeps them off the street.” – **Gus Kyle**.

11. “Some people just need a high-five to the face with a closed fist.” – **Unknown**.

12. “My dad had this thing – everyone in Canada wants to play hockey; that’s all they want to do. So, when I was a kid, whenever we skated, my dad would not let us on the ice without hockey sticks because of this insane fear we would become figure skaters!” – **Norm Macdonald**.

13. “A puck is a hard rubber disc that hockey players strike when they can’t hit one another.” – **Jimmy Cannon**.

14. “Why is a puck called a puck? Because ‘dirty little bastard’ was taken.” – **Martin Brodeur**.

15. “I don’t want to get into a ‘he said, she said’ with the refs... I’m the he.” – **Chris Pronger**.

CHAPTER 5

COLLEGE SPORTS

Trivia Questions

1. Who played in the famous 'Game of the Century' on January 2, 1987, that had the largest television audience in college football history?

2. Who made the most field goals in a single game of college football?

3. Florida State baseball coach, Mike Martin, had how many wins?

4. Between 1996 and 1998, the LSU baseball team had how many consecutive games with a home run?

5. Cael Sanderson won how many wrestling matches at Iowa State?

6. Mia Hamm, the name synonymous with women's football in the USA, represented which college?

7. What is Notre Dame's nickname?
8. Who is the only two-time winner of the Heisman Trophy?
9. Which sport first introduced the naming of an All-American team?
10. Who is in the College Football Hall of Fame and has also won an Oscar?
11. Harvard and Yale competed in the first-ever intercollegiate event in 1852. What was the event?
12. Which US college sport gives the Hobey Baker award to the best player?
13. What is the second most popular sport in college, after basketball?
14. Who played in the first Orange Bowl in 1935?
15. Which college has the most national football championships?
16. Otto the Orange is the mascot for which university?
17. When was the NCAA established?
18. Who famously coached Team USA to the 'Miracle on Ice' at the 1980 Winter Olympics, and what college did he attend?
19. Which sport is 'March Madness' associated with?
20. Which charter member of the Atlantic Coast Conference won the very first ACC Basketball Tournament in 1954?
21. Which USC standout was the first woman to win consecutive final four MVP honors?

22. Which famous author was a classmate of Hobey Baker, and which college did they attend?

23. 'The Big House' refers to the stadium that which college football team plays at?

24. Howard's Rock plays a role in a tradition for which university?

25. In a baseball game for Florida State, Marshall McDougall once had how many RBIs?

26. Which college baseball team holds the longest streak of not being shut out, and how long is the streak?

27. After Tim Tebow famously wrote "John 3:16" on his eye blacks in 2009, how many people googled the Bible verse?

28. Which NBA number 1 draft pick had their shoe explode whilst playing for Duke against their rival, UNC?

29. Who led the Clemson Tigers to a national championship against Alabama after throwing for 420 yards and three touchdowns, including the game-winning score to Hunter Renfrow with just one second remaining on the clock?

30. Famous actress, Emma Watson, played which sport whilst she studied at Brown University?

31. The award-winning movie, 'Rudy', features which famous college?

32. Which US President formed the IAAUS, now known as the NCAA, to create rules for intercollegiate sports?

33. Who was the first halfback from the SEC to ever win the Heisman Trophy (1942)?

34. Which University did Frank Sinkwich attend?

35. How many shutouts did Tennessee pitcher Monica Abbott achieve in her college career?

36. Which famous college athlete once ran for 1000 yards as a senior in only 8 games, and led the nation for goals in lacrosse (43) in 1957 at Syracuse?

37. Which US Olympic swimmer never lost a dual meet in her time at the University of California (2001-2003)?

38. Which Iowa State wrestling star has a collegiate record of 118-1?

39. The 'Air Gait' move in lacrosse was made famous by which athlete?

40. Who was named Naismith Women's Collegiate Player of the Century?

Match the mascot with the college sport

Mascot	College Sport
Sam the Minuteman	University of Massachusetts Amherst
Champ the Husky	University of Southern Maine
Donald Duck	University of Oregon
Sparky	Arizona State
Masked Rider	Texas Tech
Paydirt Pete	University of Texas at El Paso
Cosmo the Cougar	Brigham Young University
Big Green	Dartmouth
Bevo	University of Texas at Austin
Sebastian the Ibis	Miami University
Traveler	University of Southern California
Knightro	University of Central Florida
Hokie	Virginia Tech

Mascot	College Sport
Demon Deacon	Wake Forest
Nittany Lion	Pennsylvania State University
Ralphie the Buffalo	University of Colorado
Colonel Reb	Ole Miss
Chief Osceola and Renegade	Florida State University
Ramblin' Wreck	Georgia Tech
Mike the Tiger	Louisiana State University
Mountaineer	Virginia Tech
UGA	University of Georgia
Monte	University of Montana
Vili the Warrior	University of Hawaii
Baldwin the Eagle	Boston College

Top 10 Highest Attended College Football Games

1. (1.) **The Battle at Bristol** was an American college football game played at Bristol Motor Speedway in Bristol, Tennessee on Saturday, September 10, 2016, between the University of Tennessee Volunteers and the Virginia Tech Hokies. It holds the record for NCAA football's largest single-game attendance at 156,990.

2. (2.) (Officially) the Sept. 7, 2013 meeting between **Michigan and Notre Dame** at Michigan Stadium in Ann Arbor holds the record for the largest crowd, at 115,109.

3. (3.) (Unofficially, because the NCAA only began keeping records of games from 1948) there is great speculation around two games in 1927 and 1928, which featured **Notre Dame** at Chicago's Soldier Field. Reports suggest that both games had over 120 000 spectators. However, records suggest that only 99,573 and 103,081, respectively, were listed as paid.

4. The 4th to the 8th highest-attended college football games all took place at **Michigan's 'The Big House'** in Ann Arbor. The top 5 attendance records there are as follows:

5. (4.) **Notre Dame at Michigan**, Sept. 7, 2013 – 115,109.

6. (5.) **Notre Dame at Michigan**, Sept. 10, 2011 – 114,804.

7. (6.) **Ohio State at Michigan**, Nov. 26, 2011 – 114,132.

8. (7.) **Michigan State at Michigan**, Oct. 20, 2012 – 113,833.

9. (8.) **Nebraska at Michigan**, Nov. 19, 2011 – 113,718.

10. Rounding out the unofficial top 10 are games played at Beaver Stadium (featuring **Penn State vs. Nebraska**, Sept. 14, 2002, with an attendance of 110,753 people) and Kyle Field (where **Texas A&M** took on **Ole Miss** on Oct. 11, 2014, with 110,633 fans looking on).

Major College Rivalries

Football

1. Army-Navy (Navy, 61-53-7)
2. Alabama-Auburn (Alabama, 47-37-1)
3. Michigan-Ohio State (Michigan, 58-51-6)
4. Florida – Florida State
5. Ole Miss – Mississippi State

Basketball

1. Duke-North Carolina. 25 of 25
2. Louisville-Kentucky. 24 of 25
3. Kansas-Kansas State. 23 of 25

Lacrosse

1. War on the Shore – Washington College vs Salisbury University
2. Princeton University vs Rutgers University
3. Syracuse vs Virginia University
4. John Hopkins vs. Loyola (Battle of Charles Street)

Soccer

1. Indiana vs Notre Dame
2. Cal Poly vs UC Santa Barbara
3. UC Santa Barbara vs UCLA

Women's Volleyball

1. Penn State vs Pittsburgh
2. Nebraska vs Stanford
3. Southern California vs UCLA

Baseball

1. Mississippi State vs Ole Miss
2. Fullerton vs Long Beach State
3. Clemson vs South Carolina
4. Oklahoma vs Oklahoma State

Ice Hockey

1. Boston University vs Maine
2. Minnesota vs Wisconsin
3. Michigan vs Notre Dame
4. Boston vs Notre Dame

CHAPTER 6

OLYMPICS

Trivia Questions

1. Which country did the Olympics originate in?
2. When were the first games of the modern Olympic era held?
3. Where were these games held?
4. Which person started the modern Olympic Games?
5. What colors are the Olympic rings?
6. What do the Olympic rings represent?
7. Who was the first American woman to win an Olympic event?
8. Which Winter Olympics host city was the first to use artificial snow at the games?

9. Who were the athletes who famously protested against racial segregation in the 1968 Olympics?

10. The 1968 Olympic torch relay followed the path of which famous explorer?

11. The Sydney 2000 Olympics debuted which two sports?

12. Chariots of Fire tells the story of which two runners connected to the 1924 Olympic Games?

13. Snowboarding made its Olympic debut in what year?

14. Which was the first year that USA's 'Dream Team' participated in the Summer Olympics?

15. In which year was South Africa reintroduced to the Olympics for the first time since 1960?

16. In the ancient games, the Greeks would sacrifice which animal to signify the end of the games?

17. In which year did the Olympic flag debut?

18. In which year were gold, silver, and bronze medals first awarded at the Olympic Games?

19. How many countries boycotted the Moscow Olympic Games in 1980?

20. What prize was given to the winners of events in the ancient games?

21. George Eyser, who competed at the 1904 Olympic Games and won 6 gold medals, was famous for having what?

22. In 1904, which athlete was disqualified for doing a large portion of the 40-kilometre marathon race in a car?

23. Which was the first Latin American city to host the games?

24. The first women's marathon debuted during which Olympic Games?

25. Who was the first Olympian to be disqualified for testing positive for steroids?

26. Where were the first Winter Olympics held?

27. Which participating country has won at least 1 gold medal at every Summer Olympic Games?

28. Who is the only person to have lit the Olympic cauldron and won a gold medal in the same games?

29. Who was the first gold medal winner for Bermuda in the triathlon at the Tokyo games in 2021?

30. The nation of Qatar had never won a gold medal until they won two, just 1 day apart, at which games?

31. How long did the London games go on for in 1908?

32. In 1976, Canada hosted the summer games in which city?

33. Which sport in the Winter Olympics used to be a part of the Summer Olympics?

34. Which Summer Olympic Games were affected by student riots?

35. What is the name of the organization that looks after the Olympics?

36. Which country enters the Parade of Nations last at the end of the games?
37. How many athletes have won gold medals competing for two different nations?
38. In which year was tennis reinstated as an Olympic sport?
39. Which games televised women's wrestling for the first time?
40. Which is the lowest-populated country to win a medal at the Summer Olympic Games?
41. How many countries attended the 1896 Olympic Games?
42. Which Olympic event honors Pheidippides?
43. In which year were electronic timing devices used for the first time at the Olympics?
44. True or False? In the case of the modern Olympics, the Winter and Summer Olympics took place in the same year.
45. Where did the 1980 Olympics take place?
46. True or False? Hot Air Ballooning has never been an Olympic sport.
47. Which Olympics were disrupted by the 'Munich incident'.
48. Which was the first US City to host a modern Olympic Games?
49. In which year did baseball receive official event status in the Olympics?
50. Who was the first person to take the Olympic oath?

51. Which athlete, in the 1928 Olympic Games in Amsterdam, slowed down to make way for a group of ducks in the middle of a rowing race?

52. Which athlete took part in the 1904 games with a prosthetic leg, and still won a gold medal?

53. Which famous actor won 5 swimming gold medals?

54. Which athlete wore a parachute while flying to the 1960 Olympics in Rome?

55. Which country's athletes take the first position in the Parade of Nations at the opening ceremony?

56. Which Olympic Games was the first to have female representation from every single competing country?

57. Who is said to be the founder of the Special Olympics?

58. What is the motto of the Special Olympics?

59. Which USA Olympic 1977 decathlete was featured on a Wheaties cereal box, and had their own action figure?

60. In which year did surfing become an Olympic sport?

True or False?

1. Athletes in the ancient games competed naked.
2. In the 1900 Olympic Games, tug of war was one of the events.
3. The first Olympics were held to honor the Greek legend, Hercules.
4. In 1912, the Olympic Gold medals were made completely of gold.
5. Princess Anne of the UK competed in the 1976 Olympic Games.
6. The Paralympic Games began because sports were seen as an important means to help rehabilitate those who were disabled in World War II.
7. 1996 was the last time that the Summer and Winter Games were held in the same year.
8. The Obstacle Swim has never been an Olympic event.
9. The 1964 Summer Games in Tokyo were the first televised Olympics.
10. Australia hosted the first Special Olympic Games in 1968.
11. In the 1900 Olympic Games in Paris, there was a live pigeon shooting competition.
12. Synchronized swimming has been included as a solo event at the Olympic Games.
13. Dodgeball is an Olympic sport.

Facts

1. **Most personal medals ever** – Michael Phelps, USA – Swimming (28).
2. **Most gold medals in a single year** – Michael Phelps, USA – Swimming (8).
3. **Most appearances** – Ian Miller, Canada – Equestrian (10).
4. **Oldest Olympian** – Oscar Swahn, Sweden – Shooting (72 years, 281 days).
5. **Youngest Olympic medalist** – Marjorie Gestring, USA – Diving (13 years, 268 days).
6. **China** has won 28 out of a possible 32 gold medals in table tennis. The next highest gold medal winner is South Korea… with 3.
7. In 1976, Nadia Comaneci executed **6 perfect gymnastic routines** in the Olympic Games.
8. In the 1904 Games, the USA finished with **239 medals**.
9. Peter Norman received a posthumous **Order of Merit** in 2008 for his part in the 1968 medal ceremony, when he stood in solidarity with John Carlos and Tommie Smith, both of whom attended his funeral and carried his coffin.
10. The unlit **Olympic torch** has made several trips to outer space.

Match the Olympian with the country they represent

Olympian	Country
Greg Louganis	Australia
Kathy Freeman	Italy
Mary Peters	Czechoslovakia
Usain Bolt	Japan
Paavo Nurmi	Great Britain
Eric (the Eel) Moussambani	USA
Karnam Malleswari	China
Ralf Schumann	Jamaica
Valentina Vezzali	Germany
Guo Jingjing	Equatorial Guinea
Yelena Isinbayeva	Romania
Nomura Tadahiro	Ethiopia
Nadia Comaneci	Russia
Haile Gebrselassie	Finland
Emil Zatopek	India

CHAPTER 7

SOCCER

Trivia Questions

1. As of 2022, who has won the most Ballon d'Or soccer awards for best male player of the year?
2. The legendary 'Hand of God' goal was scored by who?
3. During which World Cup was the above goal scored?
4. Which World Cup made the 'Vuvuzela' famous?
5. FIFA stands for what?
6. Which country has won the most World Cups?
7. Which was the first French team to win the European champions league, in 1993?

8. Who played in the first ever European Cup Final in 1956?

9. Which English team was known as the 'Invincibles' in 2003 – 2004?

10. Which stadium's nickname is 'The Theatre of Dreams'?

11. How many times has Benfica won the European Champions League?

12. Which two club teams play at the Maracanã Stadium?

13. The A-League is the national league for which country?

14. Cristiano Ronaldo was signed to Manchester United in 2003 from which club?

15. Which famous manager signed Cristiano Ronaldo in 2003?

16. Which player controversially signed with Shanghai SIPG in the Chinese Super League from Chelsea, enjoying a record $25 million deal from 2017 through to 2020?

17. Which country is said to have invented soccer?

18. Which is the oldest known football club in the world?

19. When was the first FIFA World Cup, and which country hosted it?

20. What is the relevance of a pig's bladder to the game of soccer?

21. Bobby Zamora and Obafemi Martins are the only two players to do what in the English Premier League?

22. Which player has been substituted the most times in the English Premier League?

23. What is the highest 'official' attendance number at a world soccer match, and which stadium hosted the game?

24. In which year was Real Madrid officially founded?

25. In which year were the official rules of soccer, as we know them today, codified?

26. Which Major League Soccer team does David Beckham own?

27. What is the record number of red cards given in a single soccer game?

28. What other major international tournament was Uruguay the first to win in 1916?

29. Which two teams share the Stadio Olimpico stadium in the Serie A?

30. The 'Supporter's Shield' is an annual award in which country's national league?

31. Who was the first Peruvian player to feature in the English Premier League?

32. Which country was the first Asian nation to compete in the FIFA World Cup?

33. Spain's annual knockout cup competition goes by what name?

34. Which team has won the domestic league in the Netherlands 36 times (as of 2022)?

35. How many goals did Pele score in World Cup games?

36. Who was the only unbeaten team in the 2010 FIFA World Cup?

37. Which is the only team to win a World Cup final whilst wearing a red playing strip?

38. Which club did David Beckham play for whilst on loan from Manchester United in 1994/1995?

39. The 1968 European Championship semi-final was decided in what way?

40. Which Swedish footballer once had a clause inserted into his Premier League contract that prohibited him from travelling into space?

41. Which German international player went on to have a professional wrestling career in the WWE?

42. Which hotel did Jose Mourinho live in while he managed Manchester United?

43. What was Lionel Messi's schoolboy team?

44. Elton John has owned which English football team twice?

45. What is the name of the European Championship trophy?

46. With 365 goals, who holds the record for the top Bundesliga goal scorer of all time?

47. What colors did Manchester wear before they famously adopted red as the home color of their strip?

48. In Spanish football, what is 'the Pichichi'?

49. Which player holds the fastest hat trick in the Premier League?

50. Which 3 players have the most English Premier League red cards?

51. Who has scored the most goals in a single World Cup?

52. Which is the most attended World Cup match in history?

53. Which club was the last to beat Real Madrid in the European final?

54. Which Italian player played in 4 World Cups for the Azzurri, but never played in a single World Cup qualifier?

55. Which former Chelsea and Barcelona striker replaced his father in his international debut for Iceland at age 17?

56. Which two teams played off in the match with the smallest ever recorded attendance, at the biggest stadium to ever host a league of football?

57. Which is the only Scottish club to have reached an FA Cup final?

58. Which is the only English club to have won a major domestic honor under a sitting monarch since professional football was invented?

59. Which two prolific Dutch goal scorers were both born on 1 July 1976?

60. Which Barcelona legend won the lottery in Qatar?

Who Am I?

1. I was born in 1976 in Rio de Janeiro and played my club football at Cruzeiro, PSV Eindhoven, Barcelona, Inter Milan, Real Madrid, AC Milan, and Corinthians. I won the Ballon d'Or award for best player in the world during my time with Inter Milan, and then again with Real Madrid. I played in 3 World Cups for my native Brazil, and represented the nation on 98 occasions. I am the highest Brazilian goal scorer in World Cup history, and in the 2002 World Cup finals, I sported an unusual yet popular hairstyle to take the media attention away from my injured knee. I wore number 9 when playing for my country. Who am I?

2. Widely regarded as one of the best, if not the best player in the history of world football, I am famous for scoring the goal known as 'The Hand of God' in the 1986 World Cup quarter final against England. Known as 'El Pibe de Oro' (The Golden Boy), I had a club career that took me from the Argentinos Juniors to Boca Juniors, Barcelona, Napoli, Sevilla, Newell's Old Boys, and back to Boca Juniors. I was capped 91 times for 34 goals for my beloved Argentina and lifted the World Cup in 1986 in Mexico. Who am I?

3. FIFA labelled me player the greatest of all time, and in 1999, the International Olympic Committee named me 'Athlete of the Century'. I hold the Guinness Book of Records title for most goals in games played – 1363 games for 1279 goals. Born in Tres Coracoes, Brazil in 1940, I debuted for Santos in 1956 at just 14 years old and went on to play 636 games for the mighty Brazilian club. I was a 3-time World Cup winner in 1958, 1962, and 1970. In the 1958 final, I scored two goals and became the youngest player to play in a World Cup final. I finished my club career

playing for New York Cosmos. Many players from my era say that he was not only the best footballer but the best athlete they ever saw. My life in football has been credited to connecting the phrase 'The Beautiful Game' to football. Who am I?

4. I'm a former English striker whose signature goal celebration was to run off and hold one arm raised with a full palm in the air. This celebration was seen 148 times in 303 games for Newcastle after I started my career at Southampton before moving to Blackburn Rovers. I played 63 internationals for England, scoring 30 times along the journey. I was a prolific goal scorer who won the Premier League Golden Boot in 94/95, 95/96, and 96/97, and was named Premier League Player of the Year in 1994/95. I was a member of the Blackburn Rovers team that won the Premier League in 1994/95. I have since gone on to become a manager at my beloved Newcastle, and am a football pundit on various channels. Who am I?

5. One of the most popular footballers of all time, I became an icon of the game for both my on-field and off-field prowess. Born in London in 1975, my youth career started at Tottenham Hotspur, but it was my time at Manchester United during the golden era of Sir Alex Ferguson that saw me become a household name. I played 265 times for the Red Devils and was a part of the famous Treble winning side in 1999. I won the Premier League 6 times and the FA cup twice. I captained my country for 6 years and earned 115 international appearances. I am most famous for my set-piece expertise, and boast a highlight reel littered with goals from free kicks. Perhaps what made me most recognizable were the Adidas Predator football boots that became synonymous with my play. I went on to play for Real Madrid, La Galaxy, AC Milan, and Paris Saint Germain. I am now the owner of Inter Miami FC. Who am I?

6. My most famous moment occurred in the 2002 World Cup Final when I was sent off for head-butting Marco Materazzi. I was an attacking midfielder renowned for my elegance, vision, passing, ball control, and technique. I was FIFA World Player of the Year in 1998, 2000, and 2003, and won the Ballon d'Or in 1998. My club career consisted of 506 appearances for Cannes, Bordeaux, Juventus, and Real Madrid during the era of the 'Galacticos'. I was a World Cup winner in front of my home fans in France, in '98, and a runner-up 8 years later in Germany. I have gone on to manage Real Madrid to 3 champions league titles and 2 La Liga titles. Who am I?

7. I spent my entire club career at Roma FC. My nickname in my home country of Italy is L'Ottavo Re di Roma (The Eighth King of Rome). As a creative offensive playmaker who had a deadly goal-scoring ability, I am widely considered to be Roma's greatest-ever player. During my tenure, I won a Serie A title, two Coppa Italias, and 2 Supercoppa Italiana titles. I am the second-highest scorer of all time in Italian league history, with 250 goals. I was a 2006 FIFA World Cup winner and a finalist in Euro 2000. I was crowned Serie A Italian Footballer of the Year 5 times, and in 2011, was considered to be the most popular player in Europe. I am a true number 10 and an immortal of Italian football. Who am I?

8. Born in Amsterdam in 1969, I am a Dutch maestro who was a wide midfielder and moved forward to play as a striker later in my career. Nicknamed the 'non-flying Dutchman' by the fans of my beloved Arsenal, I played 315 times for the London club after starting my club career at Dutch superpower, Ajax, before moving to Inter Milan, and finally to Arsenal. I won 3 Premier League titles, four FA Cups, and played in the 2006 Champions League Final for Arsenal. This was to be my last appearance as a player. I was responsible for one of the greatest goals of FIFA World Cup history with a last-minute winner against Argentina in

the 1998 quarter final. I have been described as having the finest technique of any player, and Thierry Henry described me as a 'dream striker'. In 2017, I was awarded best goal in the Premier League for my goal against Newcastle United in 2002. Who am I?

9. Born March 21, 1980 in Porto Alegre, Brazil, I am seen globally as the icon of 'Joga Bonito'. A Ballon d'Or winner and 2-time FIFA player of the year winner, I started my club career at Gremio, after which it took me to Paris Saint-Germain, Barcelona, AC Milan, Flamengo, Atlético Mineiro, Queretaro, and Fluminense. I was a part of the 2002 World Cup-winning Brazilian side and wore the famous number 10. In 2020, I was imprisoned in Paraguay for tax evasion. Who am I?

10. I am a Dutch master who is considered to be one of the most influential figures in modern football, both for the way I played and for the concepts I applied during my management career. I was a 3-time Ballon d'Or winner in 1971, 1973, and 1974, and was the poster child for the concept known as Total Football, explored by Rinus Michels. I was born in Amsterdam in 1947 and played for Ajax, Barcelona, Los Angeles Aztecs, Washington Diplomats, Levante, and Feyenoord. I represented the Netherlands 48 times and scored 33 goals in the process. In the 1974 tournament, I was named FIFA player of the tournament and led the Dutch team to the final. I am famous for introducing the renowned style of play made famous in Barcelona, called 'tiki-taka', which is characterized by short passing and movement. I have gone on to manage Ajax, Barcelona, and Catalonia at a senior level, and am widely regarded as being in the top 3 footballers who ever lived. Who am I?

Match the team with their home stadium

Team	Stadium
Boca Juniors, Argentina	Allianz Arena
Ajax, Amsterdam, Netherlands	La Bombonera
AC Milan, Inter Milan, Italy	Estadio Da Luz
Bayern Munich, Germany	Wanda Metropolitano
Fluminense & Flamengo, Rio de Janeiro	Johan Cruyff Arena
River Plate, Buenos Aires, Argentina	Old Trafford
Kaiser Chiefs, Johannesburg, South Africa	Monumental
Manchester United, England	Nou Camp
Benfica, Lisbon, Portugal	Anfield
Selangor FC, Malaysia	Maracanã
Barcelona, Spain	Shah Alam Stadium
Arsenal, London, England	Soccer City Stadium
Atletico Madrid, Spain	Emirates Stadium
Liverpool, England	St. James Park
Newcastle United FC	San Siro

Match the players to the club where they made their senior team debut

Player	Club
Christiano Ronaldo	Chemnitzer FC
Michael Ballack	Tottenham Hotspur
Luka Modric	Manchester United
Raheem Sterling	Sporting Lisbon
Erling Haaland	Lyon
Lorenzo Insigne	Bryne
Paul Pogba	Boulogne
Mohamed Salah	Santos
Karim Benzema	Genk
Robert Lewandowski	Nacional
Kevin De Bruyne	Zagreb
Harry Kane	Liverpool
N'Golo Kanté	Al Mokawloon
Luis Suarez	Napoli
Neymar	Delta Warsaw

CHAPTER 8

TENNIS

Trivia Questions

1. What are the 4 tennis Grand Slams played in a calendar year?
2. True or False? Players can wear any color clothing when playing at Wimbledon.
3. Which tennis player is famous for saying, "you can't be serious"?
4. Which male player has the most singles Grand Slam titles?
5. In which tennis tournament do players represent their country in a team-based playoff?
6. What is an ace?

7. True or False? Before tennis players used rackets, people would use the palms of their hands to hit the ball back and forth over the net.
8. Which two players made up the famous doubles combination known as 'The Woodies'?
9. What color were tennis balls before they were yellow?
10. What is it called when the score is 40-40?
11. Who were the first set of sisters to win Olympic gold medals in tennis?
12. Which tennis event is played at Roland-Garros?
13. Which player has won the most consecutive women's Grand Slam titles?
14. Martina Hingis hails from which country?
15. Who defeated tennis player Bobby Riggs in the famous "Battle of the Sexes"?
16. Who did John McEnroe defeat in the final to win his first Wimbledon singles title?
17. In which year was tennis originally introduced as an Olympic sport?
18. Which six-time Grand Slam winner was jailed in the UK?
19. Which tennis player married pop sensation, Enrique Iglesias?
20. Which tennis player from the USA was ranked in the year-end top 10 for nine consecutive years?

CHAPTER 9

COMBAT SPORTS

Trivia Questions

1. Which UFC fighter was the first to hold two separate weight division championships?
2. Which female UFC fighter goes by the nickname 'Thug Rose'?
3. Which boxers fought in the famous 'Rumble in the Jungle' fight?
4. What does it mean to 'cut weight' in combat sports?
5. Who is the famous owner of the UFC?
6. GSP are the initials of which French Canadian MMA fighter?
7. Which Mixed Martial Arts discipline can be abbreviated as BJJ?

8. What does TKO stand for?
9. Which famous US fighter was known as 'The Cowboy'?
10. Which formerly homeless UFC fighter featured in Fast and the Furious 9?
11. Which boxer famously had his ear bitten off by Mike Tyson?
12. Which fictional boxer is played by Sylvester Stallone?
13. Canelo Alvarez hails from which country?
14. Tyson Fury goes by what nickname?
15. How many weight divisions are there in the UFC?
16. Which notorious Californian brothers fight out of Stockland?
17. Where is Urijah Faber's gym, 'Ultimate Fitness', located?
18. Who did Jon 'Bones' Jones defeat in his UFC debut?
19. How many times did Chuck Lidell fight in the UFC?
20. Who was the first British fighter to win a UFC championship?
21. Ronda Rousey lost to Holly Holm at UFC 193; which round did the fight end in, and how did it end?
22. True or False? Dominick Cruz's first loss in the UFC came against Cody Garbrandt.
23. How many seconds did it take Jorge Masvidal to knock out Ben Askren?

24. Which country was Lyoto Machida born in?

25. Who did Cris Cyborg beat in her UFC debut?

26. True or False? Wanderlei Silva won a title during his UFC career?

27. Which English UFC fighter is known as 'The Baddy'?

28. Who has won the most Performance bonuses in the UFC?

29. Jim Miller holds the record for the most UFC fights (as of 2022); how many times did he fight in the promotion?

30. Which retired UFC fighter lost only 1 single round in his career?

CHAPTER 10

GOLF

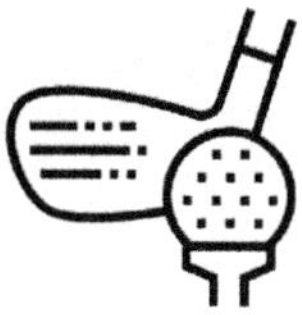

Trivia Questions

1. Which former Major winner is the face of the rogue golfing competition, 'LIV' golf?
2. What is a Bogey?
3. In which of golf's Major tournaments is the winner presented with a green jacket?
4. Who was the Solheim Cup named after?
5. What is the diameter of the hole in golf?
6. The Royal and Ancient Golf Club is the oldest golf club in the world, and is considered to be the home of golf. In which country is it found?

7. The Ryder Cup was originally contested between which two teams?
8. Which golfer won The Open Championship 5 times between 1975 and 1983?
9. What is the maximum number of golf clubs allowed in a golf bag?
10. Who was the first non-American player to win The Masters?
11. Which golfer set the record for the lowest aggregate 72-hole score in the PGA Championship, when he won the tournament with a 16 under par score of 264 in 2018?
12. Which golfer's nickname is "The Big Easy"?
13. Which golf course has been home to The Players Championship since 1982?
14. Which king of Scotland banned golf in 1457, because it interfered with military training?
15. Who is the Ryder Cup named after?
16. Where did the game of golf originate?
17. What is it called when you hit the ball and don't like where it lands, and then choose to tee off again?
18. Who is the youngest Masters champion?
19. Who was the first Masters Tournament winner?
20. What is the name given to a person who carries the golf player's bag?

True or False?

1. Golf was the first sport to be played on the moon.
2. Four shots under par is called a 'condor'.
3. The dimples on a golf ball are there to slow the ball down.
4. There are 16 holes on a regulation golf course.
5. Rory McIlroy has spent over 100 weeks as the number 1 ranked golfer in the world.
6. Nick Faldo has 75 professional golfing titles.
7. The total prize money pool for The Players Championship is $12,500,000.
8. If a player's ball strikes another player's ball on the putting green, the penalty is 3 strokes.
9. France will hold the 2022 Ryder Cup.
10. Jack Nicklaus originally planned to become a pharmacist.

CHAPTER 11

MIXED CATEGORY

Rugby Trivia

1. Which English flyhalf kicked a drop goal in the 2003 World Cup final to win the game and win the World Cup?

2. Which international rugby team is known as the Pumas?

3. Who is the youngest player to play 50 test matches for his country?

4. Who has won the European 6 Nations the most times?

5. Who won the Women's Rugby World Cup in 2017?

6. Which country famously performs the 'Haka' before their matches?

7. Which Springbok player kicked 5 drop goals against England in the 1999 World Cup?

8. Who is the all-time highest points scorer in International Rugby?

9. The Calcutta Cup is contested between which 2 countries?

10. Who has the most international caps in world rugby history?

Motorsports Trivia

1. Who won the very first Indianapolis 500?
2. What does the yellow flag mean?
3. At which track did Dale Earnhardt Jr make his first Winston Cup appearance?
4. In which state did Greg Moore tragically die in a race in 1999?
5. Which Formula 1 racing team has the nickname, 'The Prancing Horse'?
6. Which Icelandic Formula 1 World Champion has the nickname, 'The Iceman'?
7. Who is the youngest driver to win a Formula 1 race?
8. Which F1 team holds the record for most wins in a season?
9. How many F1 titles did Michael Schumacher win?
10. Which Formula 1 driver has the longest streak of victories?
11. What is the highest official speed ever reached in MotoGP?
12. In what year was the first annual MotoGP competition held?
13. In what year did Mick Doohan's career end?
14. Which country is Valentino Rossi from?
15. True or false? An average MotoGP bike is worth more than 1 million US dollars.

Surfing Trivia

1. Which surfer holds the record for being crowned world champion 11 times?
2. Where is the famous 'Pipeline' surf break located?
3. What do you call a surfer who rides with his right foot forward?
4. Which female surfer has won the most world championship titles?
5. The most famous big wave surfing event in the world, which takes place in Waimea Bay, Hawaii, is named after which surfer who lost his life in Moloka'i, Hawaii?

Aussie Rules Trivia

1. Which team has played in the most grand finals?
2. What are the two colors of match ball used by the AFL?
3. Who were the two founding clubs of the VFL (now known as the AFL)?
4. Which two teams merged to create the Brisbane Lions in 1996?
5. How many points do you get for kicking a goal in AFL?
6. True or False? Aussie Rules Football is the biggest sport in the country, based on participation.
7. How many clubs were a part of the VFL from 1925?
8. Which is the only team to have been in the competition for 1 year and won a premiership?
9. Which coach coined the phrase, 'if it bleeds, we can kill it.'?
10. Who holds the record for the most goals kicked in a game at the Gabba?

Cycling Trivia

1. How many miles does the Tour de France cover?
2. What is the proper name for a cycling track?
3. Which country does Bradley Wiggins hail from?
4. Which team did Lance Armstrong first win a Tour de France for?
5. Who has won the most stages in the Tour de France?
6. Which cycling race is the longest in the world?
7. True or False? A track cycling bike has no brakes.
8. In which decade was the Tour of Britain introduced?
9. Where was the first Road World Cycling Championships held?
10. What is the first cycling race of the year that contributes to cyclists' world rankings?
11. Which cycling classic is nicknamed, 'La Classica di Primavera'?
12. Erik Zabel is from which country?
13. Which sprinter from the Isle of Man won the 'La Primavera' (the world's longest single-day bike race) in 2009?
14. In which century was the bicycle invented?
15. The Vuelta A España race typically starts in which month of the year?

Cricket Trivia

1. Which countries contest in the coveted Ashes Tournament?
2. When was the first Indian Premier League T20 Tournament played?
3. Which Australian fast bowler was known as 'The Wild Thing'?
4. What is the South African cricket team called?
5. Which team had the most feared fast-bowling attack in the 1990s?
6. Who has the fastest-recorded delivery in history?
7. What does LBW stand for in cricket terminology?
8. Which famous businessman introduced world series cricket (the introduction of colored clothing)?
9. Which cricketer is known as 'the King of Spin'?
10. Who has scored the most one-day international runs in history?

SECTION 2

ANSWERS

Ready to settle the score?

Chapter 1: Basketball

Answers: Trivia

1. Kobe Bryant
2. 6 times: 1991, 1992, 1993, 1996, 1997, 1998
3. On Nov. 1, 1946, the New York Knickerbockers played the Toronto Huskies.
4. Earvin
5. 1979.
6. Big Ticket.
7. 22 April, 1996.
8. 1 - Boston Celtics.
9. 11
10. Wilt Chamberlain, 1962.
11. Argentina.
12. Jerry West.
13. Indiana Pacers and Detroit Pistons.
14. Michael Jordan.
15. November 1, 1946 (New York Knickerbockers VS Toronto Huskies).
16. Isiah Thomas.
17. George 'Mr Basketball' Mikan.
18. Phil Jackson (11).
19. Lew Alcindor.
20. Lebron James.
21. Minnesota Timberwolves.
22. Robert Parish - 1611 games.
23. NBA MVP - 1955/56.

24. Yao Ming.
25. 4 – Chucky Brown, Tony Massenburg, Joe Smith, Jim Jackson.
26. Boston Celtics. As of 2021/2022 – 3462.
27. Los Angeles Lakers – 58.
28. Steals.
29. Lebron James.
30. 12 Minutes.
31. The Staples Center.
32. Michael Jordan.
33. Larry Bird.
34. 15.
35. 29.
36. South Africa.
37. Vlade Divac.
38. Wurzburg, Germany.
39. Mychal Thompson (The Bahamas).
40. A soccer ball.
41. Jay Z.
42. Rick Barry (Brent, John, and Drew).
43. Baltimore Bullets.
44. Boston Celtics (1959).
45. Kwame Brown.
46. Philadelphia, Pennsylvania.
47. 1954.
48. Magic Johnson.
49. Big Smooth.
50. Shaquille O'Neal.

Answers: Drafted Players

Player	Institution
Lebron James	St Vincent – St Mary High School
Kobe Bryant	Lower Merion High School
Larry Bird	Indiana State
Charles Barkley	Auburn
Lamelo Ball	Illawarra Hawks
Michael Jordan	North Carolina University
Dennis Rodman	Southeastern Oklahoma State
Steve Nash	Santa Clara University
Tim Duncan	Wake Forest
Wilt Chamberlain	Harlem Globetrotters
Kevin Garnett	Farragut Career Academy High School
Blake Griffin	University of Oklahoma
Jerry West	West Virginia University
Shaquille O'Neal	Louisiana State University
James Harden	Arizona State University
Giannis Antetokounmpo	Filathlitikos
Dwayne Wade	Marquette University
Pau Gasol	FC Barcelona
Reggie Miller	UCLA
Ray Allen	University of Connecticut
Allen Iverson	Georgetown
Dirk Nowitzki	DJK Wurzburg
Kevin Durant	University of Texas
Andrew Bogut	University of Utah
Ben Simmons	LSU Tigers
Joel Embiid	Kansas Jayhawks

Devin Booker	Kentucky Wildcat
Jayson Tatum	Duke Blue Devils

Answers: Match the team with their owner

Team	**Owner**
Chicago Bulls	Jerry Reinsdorf
Dallas Mavericks	Mark Cuban
Charlotte Hornets	Michael Jordan
Indiana Pacers	Herbert Simon
Portland Trailblazers	Jody Allen
Orlando Magic	Dan DeVos
New Orleans Pelicans	Gayle Benson
Brooklyn Nets	Joseph Tsai
Cleveland Cavaliers	Dan Gilbert
Houston Rockets	Tilman Fertitta
Denver Nuggets	Ann Walton Kronke
Detroit Pistons	Tom Gores

Chapter 2: Baseball

Answers: Trivia

1. Mickey Mantle.
2. 2021.
3. Steal 300 bases.
4. Derek Jeter.
5. 1914 - 1935.
6. George Bradley.
7. World Series.
8. Boston Bees.
9. Jamie Moyer – 522.
10. RingCentral Coliseum – Home of the Oakland Athletics.
11. Atlanta Braves, Established in 1871.
12. Lou Gehrig – NY Yankees #4.
13. 2017.
14. Seattle. Seattle Pilots 1969.
15. Lebron James.
16. Mike Griffin.
17. True.
18. 1.
19. Red.
20. The Red Stockings.
21. Barry Bonds.
22. 162.
23. Effa Louise Manley.
24. San Francisco Giants.
25. Boston Red Sox.

26. Jocko.
27. Albert Belle - 1995.
28. Reggie Jackson.
29. Babe Ruth.
30. Jim Kaat.
31. 8.
32. Pilots.
33. Casey Stengel.
34. New York Yankees.
35. Milwaukee Brewers.
36. 1969.
37. Boston Beaneaters.
38. New York Giants.
39. Sammy Sosa.
40. Don Larsen.
41. 1961.
42. Take Me Out to the Ballgame – Frank Sinatra & Gene Kelly.
43. Sandy Koufax – 36 years old.
44. Lauren Boden.
45. New York Yankees.
46. The Expos.
47. Playing 2,632 consecutive games.
48. Jamie Moyer – 49 years old.
49. 108.
50. He was the first African American to play Major League Baseball in the United States.

Answers: Match the Major League Team (MLB) with their former stadium

Stadium Name	Team
The Ballpark in Arlington	Texas Rangers
Turner Field	Atlanta Braves
Memorial Stadium	Baltimore Orioles
Ebbets Field	Brooklyn Dodgers
Comiskey Park	Chicago White Sox
Veterans Stadium	Philadelphia Phillies
Three Rivers Stadium	Pittsburgh Pirates
Busch Memorial Stadium	St Louis Cardinals
Candlestick Park	San Francisco Giants
Kingdome	Seattle Mariners
Griffith Stadium	Washington Senators
Shea Stadium	New York Mets

Answers: Hollywood at the Ballpark - Match the movie with the Baseball team

Movie Title	Team
61*	New York Yankees
For Love of the Game	Detroit Tigers
The Rookie	Tampa Bay Devil Rays
Moneyball	Oakland A's
42	Brooklyn Dodgers

Major League	Cleveland Indians
The Natural	New York Knights
Rookie of the Year	Chicago Cubs
Trouble With the Curve	Atlanta Braves
Field of Dreams	Chicago White Sox

Answers: True or False

1. True.
2. True.
3. False.
4. False.
5. True.
6. True.
7. False.
8. False.
9. True.
10. True.

Chapter 3: American Football

Answers: Trivia

1. New England Patriots & Pittsburgh Steelers – 6 times.
2. National Football League.
3. Indianapolis Colts.
4. 14.
5. 4. Steelers, Raiders, Patriots, Buccaneers.
6. The Washington Redskins had a 72-point game in 1966.
7. The American Football Conference (AFC) and the National Football Conference (NFC).
8. The Miami Dolphins – 1972.
9. The New York Titans.
10. Jay Berwanger – 1936 by the Philadelphia Eagles.
11. 2010.
12. 102.4.
13. Detroit Lions.
14. Number of receptions, holding 1,549.
15. 1967.
16. 32.
17. The Miami Dolphins.
18. Colin Kaepernick.
19. Denver Broncos, New York Jets, New England Patriots, and Philadelphia Eagles (he was also contracted by the Jacksonville Jaguars for a preseason).
20. True.
21. Patrick Mahomes.
22. 64 yards.

23. Minnesota Vikings.
24. The Rams.
25. Baltimore Colts.
26. Boston.
27. 1968.
28. 18.
29. Memphis.
30. Seattle Seahawks.
31. Jerry Jones.
32. The Blind Side.
33. Lawrence Taylor.
34. Dallas Cowboys.
35. The Portsmouth Spartans, in 1930.
36. Chicago Bears.
37. Philadelphia Eagles.
38. Cleveland Browns.
39. Arizona Cardinals.
40. 40 Days.

Answers: Match the players with their teams

Player	Team
Myles Garrett	Cleveland Browns
Sam Bradford	St Louis Rams
Steve Emtman	Indianapolis Colts
Jadeveon Clowney	Houston Texans
Bo Jackson	Tampa Bay Buccaneers
O.J. Simpson	Buffalo Bills

Kenneth Sims	New England Patriots
Terry Bradshaw	Pittsburgh Steelers
Troy Aikman	Dallas Cowboys
Billy Cannon	Los Angeles Rams

Answers: Match the players with their nicknames

Player	Nickname
'Minister of Defense'	Reggie White
'The Golden Arm'	John Unitas
'Sweetness'	Walter Payton
'Joe Cool'	Joe Montana
'Night Train'	Dick Lane
'The Galloping Ghost'	Red Grange
'Mercury'	Eugene Morris
'Prime Time'	Deion Sanders
'Ironhead'	Craig Heyward
'Broadway Joe'	Joe Namath
'Honey Badger'	Tyrann Mathieu
'Beast Mode'	Marshawn Lynch
'The Refrigerator'	William Perry
'Machine Gun'	Jim Kelly
'The Alabama Antelope'	Don Hutson

Answers: Match the celebrities with the teams they root for

Celebrity	Team
Blake Shelton	Arizona Cardinals
Samuel L. Jackson	Atlanta Falcons
Michael Phelps	Baltimore Ravens

Shooter McGavin
Stephen 'Steph' Curry
Barack Obama
George Clooney
Elvis Presley
Demi Lovato
Jessica Biel
Eminem
Ellen DeGeneres
Simone Biles
Rob Lowe
Bill Murray
Paul Rudd
Ice Cube
Chuck Liddell
Ty Burrell
Johnny Depp
Josh Duhamel
Mark Wahlberg
Brad Pitt
Hugh Jackman
Ray Romano
Kevin Hart
Frank Sinatra
Jeremy Renner
J.K. Rowling
John Cena
Faith Hill & Tim McGraw
Matthew McConaughey

Buffalo Bills
Carolina Panthers
Chicago Bears
Cincinnati Bengals
Cleveland Browns
Dallas Cowboys
Denver Broncos
Detroit Lions
Green Bay Packers
Houston Texans
Indianapolis Colts
Jacksonville Jaguars
Kansas City Chiefs
Las Vegas Raiders
Los Angeles Chargers
Los Angeles Rams
Miami Dolphins
Minnesota Vikings
New England Patriots
New Orleans Saints
New York Giants
New York Jets
Philadelphia Eagles
Pittsburgh Steelers
San Francisco 49ers
Seattle Seahawks
Tampa Bay Buccaneers
Tennessee Titans
Washington Football Team

Chapter 4: Ice Hockey

Answers: Trivia

1. Stan Mikita.
2. Detroit. October 8, 1993.
3. The Boston Bruins defeated the Philadelphia Flyers 2-1 in overtime at Fenway Park on Jan. 1, 2010.
4. 26 November 1917, in Montreal, Canada.
5. 11 Teams.
6. 4.
7. Martin Brodeur.
8. Canada.
9. Toronto, Canada.
10. With a faceoff.
11. Slashing.
12. Five for Fighting.
13. The best goalie in the NHL.
14. A goal, a fight, and an assist.
15. When a player tries to slow their opponent down using their stick.
16. 3 seconds.
17. Willie O'Ree for the Bruins.
18. Seattle Kraken.
19. Gary Bettman.
20. Bobby Hull.
21. 1930.
22. Ottawa Senators.
23. Buffalo Sabres, Taro Tsujimoto.
24. 20 Rounds.

25. Mike Milbury.
26. 97; the first player in history to do so.
27. 2004.
28. True.
29. Leaes (leaves), Bqstqn (Boston).
30. Toronto Maple Leafs, 1962.
31. 6.

Answers: Match the A-listers with the teams they root for

Celebrity	**Team they support**
Will Ferrell, Cuba Gooding Jr	Los Angeles Kings
Justin Bieber	Toronto Maple Leafs
Celine Dion	Montreal Canadiens
Kristen Bell	Detroit Red Wings
Tim Robbins	New York Rangers
Alice Cooper	Arizona Coyotes
Metallica	San Jose Sharks
Chad Michael Murray	Buffalo Sabres
Vince Vaughn	Chicago Blackhawks
Brett Kissell	Edmonton Oilers
Chris Jericho	Winnipeg Jets
Russell Crowe	Pittsburgh Penguins
Billy Joel	New York Islanders
Larry King	Washington Capitals
Adam Sandler	Boston Bruins
Evander Holyfield	Carolina Hurricanes
Keith Urban, Carrie Underwood	Nashville Predators
Dwayne "The Rock" Johnson	Florida Panthers
Stephen King	Tampa Bay Lightning

John Elway	Colorado Avalanche
Patrick Mahomes	St Louis Blues
Gordon Ramsay	Vegas Golden Knights
Katy Perry	Minnesota Wild
Michael Buble	Vancouver Canucks
Jason Momoa	Calgary Flames
Macklemore	Seattle Kraken
Erin Andrews	Columbus Blue Jackets
George W. Bush	Dallas Stars
Milo Ventimiglia	Anaheim Ducks
Kate Hudson	New Jersey Devils
Matthew Perry	Ottawa Senators
Sylvester Stallone	Philadelphia Flyers

Chapter 5: College Sports

Answers: Trivia

1. No. 1 Miami Hurricanes battled the undefeated and No. 2 Penn State Nittany Lions in the Fiesta Bowl for the national championship. (Watched in 21.9 million homes).
2. Mike Prindle, Western Mich. vs. Marshall, Sept. 29, 1984 (7 made from 9 attempts).
3. 2029.
4. 77 games.
5. 159; all of them are consecutive.
6. North Carolina Tar Heels.
7. The Fighting Irish.
8. Archie Griffin of Ohio State, who won the award in both 1974 and 1975.
9. Football, starting in 1889.
10. Irvine Warburton was an All-American at the University of Southern California and won an Oscar for his editing of the movie 'Mary Poppins' in 1964.
11. A boat race.
12. Ice Hockey.
13. Cross Country.
14. University of Miami and Manhattan University.
15. Yale with 18. The last came in 1927.
16. Syracuse.
17. 1906.
18. Herbert Paul Brooks Jr. – University of Minnesota.
19. Basketball.

20. NC State.
21. Cheryl Miller.
22. F. Scott Fitzgerald – Princeton.
23. Michigan Wolverines.
24. Clemson Tigers.
25. 16.
26. Arizona State, 506 games.
27. 94 million.
28. Zion Williamson.
29. Deshaun Watson.
30. Field Hockey.
31. Notre Dame.
32. President Roosevelt in 1906.
33. Frank Sinkwich.
34. The University of Georgia.
35. 112.
36. Jim Brown – Hall of Famer in both sports.
37. Natalie Coughlan.
38. Dan Gable.
39. Gary Gait, Syracuse.
40. Chamique Holdsclaw.

Answers: Match the mascot with the college sport

Mascot	College Sport
Sam The Minuteman	University of Massachusetts Amherst
Champ the Husky	University of Southern Maine
Donald Duck	University of Oregon
Sparky	Arizona State

Masked Rider	Texas Tech
Paydirt Pete	University of Texas at El Paso
Cosmo the Cougar	Brigham Young University
Big Green	Dartmouth
Bevo	University of Texas at Austin
Sebastian the Ibis	Miami University
Traveler	University of Southern California
Knightro	University of Central Florida
Hokie	Virginia Tech
Demon Deacon	Wake Forest
Nittany Lion	Pennsylvania State University
Ralphie the Buffalo	University of Colorado
Colonel Reb	Ole Miss
Chief Osceola and Renegade	Florida State University
Ramblin' Wreck	Georgia Tech
Mike the Tiger	Louisiana State University
Mountaineer	Virginia Tech
UGA	University of Georgia
Monte	University of Montana
Vili the Warrior	University of Hawaii
Baldwin the Eagle	Boston College

Chapter 6: Olympics

Answers: Trivia

1. Greece.
2. 1896.
3. Athens, Greece.
4. Baron Pierre de Coubertin.
5. Red, blue, black, yellow, green.
6. The continents of Asia, Africa, Europe, The Americas, and Oceania.
7. Margaret Abbott - Golf.
8. Lake Placid, NY, 1980.
9. Tommie Smith and John Carlos.
10. Christopher Columbus.
11. Triathlon and taekwondo.
12. Eric Liddell and Harold Abrahams.
13. 1998.
14. 1992 - Barcelona.
15. 1992.
16. Oxen.
17. 1920.
18. 1904.
19. 66.
20. An olive crown.
21. A wooden leg.
22. Fred Lorz.
23. Mexico City.
24. Los Angeles, 1984.
25. Ben Johnson.

26. Chamonix, France – 1924.
27. Great Britain.
28. Cathy Freeman, 400m, Sydney 2000 Olympics.
29. Flora Duffy.
30. Tokyo, 2021.
31. 188 days.
32. Montreal.
33. Figure skating.
34. 1968, Mexico City.
35. IOC – International Olympic Committee.
36. The host nation.
37. 3 athletes have won gold medals competing for 2 different countries.
38. 1988.
39. Athens, 2004.
40. Bermuda.
41. 12.
42. The marathon.
43. 1912.
44. True – 1924.
45. Moscow, Russia.
46. False.
47. 1972.
48. St. Louis.
49. 1992.
50. Victor Boin.
51. Bobby Pearce.
52. George Eyser.
53. Johnny Weissmuller.
54. Muhammad Ali.
55. Greece.

56. 2012 London Games.
57. Eunice Kennedy Shriver.
58. "Let me win. But if I cannot win, let me be brave in the attempt."
59. Bruce Jenner.
60. 2020.

Answers: True or False

1. True.
2. True.
3. False.
4. True.
5. True.
6. True.
7. False. 1992 was the last time.
8. False.
9. True.
10. False. It was the USA that hosted the first Special Olympics in 1968.
11. True.
12. True.
13. False.

Answers: Match the Olympian with the country they represent

Olympian	**Country**
Greg Louganis	USA
Kathy Freeman	Australia
Mary Peters	Great Britain
Usain Bolt	Jamaica

Paavo Nurmi	Finland
Eric (the Eel) Moussambani	Equatorial Guinea
Karnam Malleswari	India
Ralf Schumann	Germany
Valentina Vezzali	Italy
Guo Jingjing	China
Yelena Isinbayeva	Russia
Nomura Tadahiro	Japan
Nadia Comaneci	Romania
Haile Gebrselassie	Ethiopia
Emil Zatopek	Czechoslovakia

Chapter 7: Soccer

Answers: Trivia

1. Lionel Messi – 6.
2. Diego Maradona.
3. 1986 in Mexico.
4. South Africa, 2010.
5. Internationale de Football Association.
6. Brazil – 5.
7. Marseille (they defeated AC Milan).
8. Real Madrid vs Stade Reims.
9. Arsenal.
10. Manchester United.
11. 2.
12. Flamingo & Fluminense (Brazil).
13. Australia.
14. Sporting Lisbon (Portugal).
15. Sir Alex Ferguson.
16. Oscar.
17. China – 1697 BCE.
18. Sheffield Football Club.
19. Uruguay, 1930.
20. Before 1855, the inner lining of a soccer ball was made from a pig's bladder.
21. Score a penalty with both their left and right feet.
22. Ryan Giggs – 134.
23. Maracanã Stadium, Rio De Janeiro, Brazil – official attendance: 199,854 – Brazil vs Uruguay.

24. 1902.
25. 1863.
26. Inter Miami F.C.
27. 36 – in 2011, referee Damien Rubino set a world record by giving out thirty-six (36) red cards in a single match between Claypole and Victoriano Arenas. After a brawl erupted, Rubino sent off all 22 players, every substitute, and some technical staff.
28. Copa America
29. Lazio & AS Roma.
30. USA – Major League Soccer.
31. Nobby Solano – 1998 for Newcastle United.
32. Indonesia – 1938.
33. Copa del Rey.
34. Ajax.
35. 12 from 14 matches.
36. New Zealand.
37. England, 1966.
38. Deepdale.
39. With a coin toss. Italy defeated the Soviet Union in the coin toss and then went on to win the final.
40. Stefan Schwarz – Sunderland, 1998.
41. Tim Wiese.
42. The Lowry Hotel.
43. Newell's Old Boys.
44. Watford.
45. Henri Delaunay Trophy.
46. Gerd Muller.
47. Green and gold.
48. The award given to the top goal scorer (named after Rafael "Pichichi" Moreno).

49. Sadio Mane – 2 minutes and 56 seconds for Southampton vs Aston Villa in 2015.
50. Patrick Vierra, Richard Dunne, and Duncan Ferguson.
51. Just Fontaine.
52. 1950 World Cup Final, Brazil vs Uruguay – 173 850 in attendance at Maracanã.
53. Aberdeen in 1983.
54. Guiseppe Bergomi.
55. Eider Gudjohnson.
56. Thames AFC vs Luton Town at Westham Stadium (469 people in attendance).
57. Queen's Park Rangers.
58. Sunderland.
59. Patrick Kluivert and Ruud van Nistelrooy.
60. Xavi.

Answers: Who am I?

1. Ronaldo (Brazil)
2. Maradona
3. Pele
4. Alan Shearer
5. David Beckham
6. Zinedine Zidane
7. Francesco Totti
8. Denis Bergkamp
9. Ronaldinho
10. Johan Cruyff

Answers: Match the team with their home stadium

Team	Stadium
Boca Juniors, Argentina	La Bombonera
Ajax, Amsterdam, Netherlands	Johan Cruyff Arena
AC Milan, Inter Milan, Italy	San Siro
Bayern Munich, Germany	Allianz Arena
Fluminense & Flamengo, Rio de Janeiro	Maracanã
River Plate, Buenos Aires, Argentina	Monumental
Kaiser Chiefs, Johannesburg, South Africa	Soccer City Stadium
Manchester United, England	Old Trafford
Benfica, Lisbon, Portugal	Estadio Da Luz
Selangor FC, Malaysia	Shah Alam Stadium
Barcelona, Spain	Nou Camp
Arsenal, London, England	Emirates Stadium
Atletico Madrid, Spain	Wanda Metropolitano
Liverpool, England	Anfield
Newcastle United FC	St. James Park

Answers: Match the players to the club where they made their senior team debut

Player	Club
Christiano Ronaldo	Sporting Lisbon
Michael Ballack	Chemnitzer FC

Luka Modric	Dinamo Zagreb
Raheem Sterling	Liverpool
Erling Haaland	Bryne
Lorenzo Insigne	Napoli
Paul Pogba	Manchester United
Mohamed Salah	Al Mokawloon
Karim Benzema	Lyon
Robert Lewandowski	Delta Warsaw
Kevin De Bruyne	Genk
Harry Kane	Tottenham Hotspur
N'Golo Kanté	Boulogne
Luis Suarez	Nacional
Neymar	Santos

Chapter 8: Tennis

Answers: Trivia

1. Australian Open, US Open, French Open, Wimbledon.
2. False – They are only permitted to play wearing the color white.
3. John McEnroe.
4. Rafael Nadal has won an all-time men's record of 22 major singles titles.
5. The Davis Cup.
6. An ace is a serve that successfully lands in the service box and does not touch the receiving player's racquet.
7. True.
8. Todd Woodbridge and Mark Woodforde.
9. White.
10. Deuce.
11. Venus and Serena Williams.
12. The French Open.
13. Serena Williams.
14. Switzerland.
15. Billy Jean King.
16. Björn Borg.
17. 1896.
18. Boris Becker.
19. Anna Kournikova.
20. Andy Roddick.

Chapter 9: Combat Sports

Answers: Trivia

1. Conor McGregor.
2. Rose Namajunas.
3. George Foreman and Muhammad Ali.
4. When a fighter deliberately loses weight to pass their weigh-in.
5. Dana White.
6. Georges St-Pierre.
7. Brazilian Jiu-Jitsu.
8. Technical Knock Out.
9. Donald Cerrone.
10. Francis Ngannou.
11. Evander Holyfield.
12. Rocky.
13. Mexico.
14. The Gypsy King.
15. 8 for males and 4 for females.
16. Nate and Nick Diaz.
17. Sacramento.
18. André Gusmão by way of a unanimous decision.
19. 23.
20. Michael Bisping.
21. Holly Holm knocked out Ronda Rousey in the 2nd round.
22. True.
23. 5 seconds.
24. Brazil.
25. Leslie Smith.

26. False.
27. Paddy Pimblett.
28. Anderson Silva – 14 bonuses.
29. 40 fights.
30. Khabib Nurmagomedov.

Chapter 10: Golf

Answers: Trivia

1. Greg Norman.
2. A score of one shot over par on a hole.
3. The Masters.
4. It is named after the Norwegian-American golf club manufacturer Karsten Solheim.
5. 4.25 inches.
6. Scotland – St Andrews.
7. Great Britain and the United States.
8. Tom Watson.
9. 14.
10. Gary Player in 1961.
11. Brooks Koepka.
12. Ernie Els.
13. TPC at Sawgrass.
14. King James II.
15. Samuel Ryder.
16. The Netherlands.
17. Mulligan.
18. Tiger Woods.
19. Horton Smith.
20. Caddy.

Answers: True or False

1. True.
2. True.

3. False.
4. False.
5. True.
6. False.
7. True.
8. False.
9. False.
10. True.

Chapter 11: Mixed Category

Answers: Rugby Trivia

1. Johnny Wilkinson.
2. Argentina.
3. Vasil Lobzhanidze for Georgia.
4. England.
5. England.
6. New Zealand.
7. Jannie De Beer.
8. Dan Carter – New Zealand.
9. England and Scotland.
10. Richie McCaw.

Answers: Motorsport Trivia

1. Ray Harroun – 1911.
2. Caution.
3. Charlotte.
4. California.
5. Ferrari.
6. Kiki Raikkonen.
7. Max Verstappen for Red Bull at age 18.
8. Mercedes – 2016, 19 out of 21.
9. 7.
10. Sebastian Vettel – 2013, 9 consecutive races.
11. 217 miles per hour.
12. 1949.
13. 1999.

14. Italy.
15. True.

Answers: Surfing Trivia

1. Kelly Slater.
2. Hawaii.
3. Goofy.
4. Stephanie Gilmore.
5. Eddie Aikau.

Answers: Aussie Rules Trivia

1. Collingwood.
2. Red and yellow.
3. Melbourne and Geelong.
4. Fitzroy Lions and Brisbane Bears.
5. 6.
6. True.
7. 12.
8. Essendon.
9. Leigh Matthews – Brisbane Lions.
10. Billy Brownless – 11 goals for Geelong.

Answers: Cycling Trivia

1. 2,068 miles.
2. Velodrome.
3. United Kingdom.
4. US Postal Service.
5. Eddy Merckx.
6. RAAM – Race Across America – 4860 km.

7. True.
8. 1940s.
9. Nurburgring, Germany.
10. Tour Down Under.
11. Milan-San Remo.
12. Germany.
13. Mark Cavendish.
14. 19th.
15. August.

Answers: Cricket Trivia

1. England and Australia.
2. 2007.
3. Shaun Tait.
4. The Proteas.
5. West Indies.
6. Shoaib Akhtar.
7. Leg before wicket.
8. Kerry Packer.
9. Shane Warne.
10. Sachin Tendulkar.

Image Credits

The interiors of this book have been designed using images from Flaticon.com

- Basketball icon: prettycons | flaticon.com/free-icon/basketball-ball_889289
- Baseball icon: justicon | flaticon.com/baseball_2279419
- Americal Football icon: Freepik | flaticon.com/free-icon/american-football_2813798
- NHL / World Hockey icon: mangsaabguru | flaticon.com/free-icon/hockey_2509966
- College Sports icon: Freepik | flaticon.com/free-icon/college-pennant_78430
- Olympics icon: Freepik | flaticon.com/free-icon/torch_1021165
- Soccer icon: Freepik | flaticon.com/free-icon/soccer-ball-variant_33736
- Tennis icon: Freepik | flaticon.com/free-icon/tennis-racket_625322
- Combat Sports icon: Eucalyp | flaticon.com/free-icon/boxing-gloves_7397018
- Golf icon: Freepik | flaticon.com/free-icon/golfing_3271038
- Mixed Category icon: Smashicons | flaticon.com/free-icon/cricket_2160173

Printed in Great Britain
by Amazon

34870535R00076